A Near Country

POEMS OF LOSS

For Robert
with thanks
for winding up
the poetry on
me.
Love,
Glenna
November 17, 199[illegible]

I love your beautiful
book!

A Near Country

POEMS OF LOSS

GLENNA LUSCHEI
DAVID OLIVEIRA
JACKSON WHEELER

SOLO PRESS
Carpinteria, California

Solo Press, 5146 Foothill Road, Carpinteria, California 93013

ISBN 0-941490-34-3 (signed limited)

ISBN 0-941490-35-1 (paperback)

Manufactured in the United States of America

First Edition

Editorial Assistant: Dana Yudovin
Book Designer: Laura Davison

Photograph of Glenna Luschei: Bill Horton
Photograph of David Oliveira: Steve Zambrano, Jr.
Photograph of Jackson Wheeler: Lee McCarthy

Photograph of the bridge at Waterloo Village, New Jersey: David Oliveira

Acknowledgements

The authors wish to thank the editors of the following publications, in which many of these poems first appeared.

Glenna Luschei:
Art/Life, Blue Mesa, Caprice, Day Break, North Stone Review, Pembroke, rivertalk

David Oliveira:
The Evergreen Chronicles, Pangolin, rivertalk, Beyond the Valley of the Contemporary Poets (The Sacred Beverage Press), *The Geography of Home: California and the Poetry of Place* (Heyday Books)

Jackson Wheeler:
Art/Life, Café Solo, rivertalk, VERVE, Swimming Past Iceland (Mille Grazie Press), *Beyond the Valley of the Contemporary Poets* (The Sacred Beverage Press)

Table of Contents

Introduction

From Santa Barbara and beyond, where the vines ripen above the sea—we have this harvest of dark fruit, this dark wine. The poets, Glenna Luschei, Jackson Wheeler, David Oliveira are elegiac in varying degrees—death shadows this harvest, but the tone of subdued celebration, subdued hunger and thirst, tender and quiet joy, suffuses all that they write.

I am moved by Glenna Luschei's bold, painterly glimpses of vibrant life. "It is bad luck to ask how we deserve this perfection," she says—and arranges her tables and postcards and gardens and photographs so that we see this perfection disappearing before us. I am moved by Jackson Wheeler's stark and powerful elegies. Their litanies, their unsparing questions, their eloquent memories from which the poet refuses to turn away, breathing "silence," seem to me among the best examples we have of the poems of grief. David Oliveira's poems, unraveling in floating "verse-talk," move me and make me humble in the presence of such grief and bounty.

I feel a sense of privilege reading these poems, as if I've wandered into a sacred place, a hushed meadow where "the trees tell us their names." David Oliveira is a wise and tender poet, as are his companions here. I am delighted to have been invited to enter their charmed space, their grief, their tenderness. I hope other readers will sip the dark wine, as I have, with thanks.

Carol Muske

Horse Latitudes

Glenna Luschei

For Linda Glenn Luschei and her brothers and sisters who miss her
Erich, Tom, and Gabriela
Theresa, Kathy, and Susan

Glenna Luschei

Glenna Luschei grew up on the Missouri River in Iowa, where her parents were corn and soya bean farmers. She has been a grower all her life, now of avocados on the Carpinteria coast in California. As she states "Because every farmer like every other gambler has to have a steady job, I have also been a poet all my life."

Luschei is the recipient of a writer's grant from the National Endowment for the Arts, a YM-YWHA Poetry Discovery Award in NYC, and the D.H. Lawrence and Wurlitzer Fellowships in Taos, New Mexico.

Over the last thirty years she has been published in many books, chapbooks, and special editions including: *Matriarch* (The Smith); *Unexpected Grace* (Turkey Press); *Back Into My Body and New Poems* (Mille Grazie Press); *Pianos Around the Cape* (Aspermont Press); and she is featured in the anthology *The Geography of Home* (Heyday Books). She is also a translator of Portuguese and Spanish authors, principally, Góngora.

Luschei divides her time between California and North Carolina where she has recently offered readings in North Wilkesboro, Winston-Salem, The University of North Carolina at Chapel Hill and St. Andrews Presbyterian College.

Of the many explanations for "Horse Latitudes," the one that resonates most with me, gives this name to the area of wild rolling seas between two belts of calm in the Tierra del Fuego of Cape Horn, where sailors once threw horses overboard in a desperate attempt to keep their ships afloat. Perhaps, what is terrifying for us is the calm after we have lost what was precious to us, and before we see what is coming next. The most staggering period is when we feel loss approaching, but we cannot forestall it. All we can do is just live through it. That's what courage is—living through.

All of these calms and roilings are territories of pain—*A Near Country* of the heart—that seem to me to yield up, finally, their own secrets and joys. All of us at one time or another explore this country. We know somehow that loss carries the seed for new growth. We muster the energy and courage to continue on. We hope you will find your own poems for healing, for living through, in this collection.

— *Glenna Luschei*

Stage

For every stage
there's a vocabulary.
Take now. Retirement.

The black waters of the St. Johns River
and your learning to hook
a minnow through the eye,

hard as going out looking
for your first job.

Your ecology is always
shifting, everglades so flooded
the owls can't find mice.
          They eat the song birds.
Anhinga drying.

The next stage
is harder than you think.
Take Florida, barely enough ground
to walk on.

Waterways

Crossing the border
doesn't seem difficult at all.
On an overcast morning
you drive to the Welcome Center
beneath the palmetto
and the rain trees.
Hands out for the glass
of mango juice,
with all humanity.

A dash of Key Lime
on the Florida line.

All of it lies ahead.
How strange to join the shiny
jointed alligator—
tin man,
lolling beneath the black waters.

It's not too bad to live again,
to embrace the yielding, hefty manatee.
Fin like the boat's motor,
sigh like the motor.
You hear him before you discover
his nostrils
snorting like hot air balloons.

It's not difficult to sleep again,
to breathe easy with the manatee.
On Alexander Springs Run
you enter the tributary.

Fellowship

It's almost New
Year's Eve
and I haven't done my life yet
still stuck on that year
as graduate student
on fellowship.

My German roommate
taught me to make glu wine
and cook calves' brain. Mein Gott!
We invited our professors to parties.
They drank from our tooth brush glasses.
She told me about her town in Germany
where Schiller lived in a tower.
Every time I bought a new dress
she got one like it, smaller.
I took her home with me to Iowa.
After doing her laundry
she complained my mother's detergent
ruined her sweaters.
Mother said German dyes are inferior.
French sauces disguise bad meat.

Her father was a merchant.
Mine sold lumber.
We deplored commerce.
We would marry artists, writers.
I read Erich Maria Remarque,
sat in on German classes.

My true love, the soldier in Germany,
sent me a compact
with edelweiss
on umbre. He scratched in my name.
Delicate
but I was out for big game.

I married the man with posture
who told me I needed an anchor
when what I craved was ballast.
I threw the urine bottle
into the Platte River.
I wasn't pregnant after all.
Too late!
I'd given up my fellowship.
Calamity kept us together eighteen years.

Here it is New Year's Eve
and I haven't caught the sadness
when she came to visit my new marriage.
She used up every fellowship. Fulbright
Danforth,
now supported herself
as potter.
At fifty she would go forth.
All these years with a married man.
He paid for the abortion.

It's nearly the stroke of twelve.
I'll never get it done.
I'll have to leave it unclosed
like the other episodes.
I took the train through Ulm,
saw her family's motorwork sign,
the town hall
with its procession of elves,
the tower where the poet pined.
I didn't call. Too late.

Summer Afternoon

Although we agree with you in anything else, Henry James,
we can't believe that "summer afternoons" are the two most delicious
words in the English language.
Summer is better after the Dog Days when the first narcissus
push up like rake tines.

We know why you said it, wickets on the lawn of Lamb House.
After croquet and tea you had time for the leisurely bath and the
white flannels for attending your 250th dinner party of the year.

What about us? Women suffer at our nadir in the summer afternoon,
most susceptible to the men who will steal our fortunes,
who will seduce us
into sending them to Europe instead of ourselves,
into raising and educating their children although we have none,
who turn never earning a dime into a matter of pride.

You said women can write about everything, even war.
You understood women
but do you understand the swoon in that summer afternoon
when women lose their astringent sensibilities, when they forget
the sacred rage, when being someone on whom nothing is lost
becomes lost in the arms of a man?

Stem

Straight as the star pine
she stood by the manger scene.
In her ribbed green blouse
she was a stem,
her hips an
amaryllis bulb,
her face the blazing flower.
She survived the double mastectomy
and thrived.

I thought of the nipple-pink
lily they call Naked Lady.
This woman was naked
to truth and passion.
"I want to dance!"
Through midnight
men lined up to dance with her.
Irresistible!

Candles leap up.
The Christmas tree,
a soldier with medals,
bows to a partner.
We fly to the forest
beneath Sagittarius,
tree and wind and star
in arabesque.
We dance, dance.
"Give me life, life."

Horse Latitudes

Over the left breast
the technician sounded the wand.
Monitors revealed loping waves,
the horse's mane and fetlock.
There! The hoof.
The black hole, the pit, days in the shallows
when we threw the horses overboard.

Couldn't we throw her overboard?
She must be excised, this foreign object,
without wounding the body.

She brought him passion
fruit vines to plant in our garden.
That transgression—
something foreign duplicated
in my marriage.
I saw her kiss him over and over
each kiss a shaft through my heart.
Something smothered the garden,
grew in my breast,
purple and oblong.
Passion fruit—anemone within my ribs.
Tentacles fibrillate in tide pools.
Beware the trap!

He dreamed he was sleeping
with a lioness in his mother's house.
"Loving, but wild, unpredictable."
I dreamed I was pacing in a cage.
He said I was the lioness.
I said it was she
or the passion fruit
growth within my breast.

I claimed myself Amazon, one breast strong,
one breast weak.
Gone.

My Last Poem to Grief

At last I take off my shoes
enter the Blue Mosque
with its six minarets.
You begged me to sail to Istanbul
with you, come to this mosque
where in the days of the Sultan
the attendants all wore blue.
Once blue carpets covered the tile.
Umber stained-glass windows remain.

All blue.

In my airport dream
I see you passing through security
with your excellent posture.
You carry my blue suitcase.
I release that baggage now.
We're both pilgrims,
both safe. I send up my poem to grief.

Outside in the Hippodrome, Turks play
on the pipes, offer raki to the tourists.
The cobras rise.
I, Kokopelli
let the songs burst forth from my haunch.
Poems coil into sweet air
from the Rio Grande to the Bosphorus.

That Summer in Lisboa

We opened the *janelas*
above tiled rooftops and the statue.
On the seventh floor where those chortling
navigators could sail away
with my pearls in their beaks
or a crust of *pão* from the *mesa,*
we left those windows wide open.

Afternoons we hiked to the beer garden
among the Diadora cedars
whose branches leave shutters wide open.
The sign said "*Há caracois*"
so we ordered sea snails and ate them
with a toothpick.

Evenings we climbed to *Bairro Alto*,
listened to the *fado*.
We took the funicular down.
Home safe.

Is it bad luck to ask
how we deserve this perfection,
a grace
from leaving the windows wide open.

Shingles

After a week of rain
the sky sails high as a parakeet.

I climb the ladder
to my roof.
Rat tat tat
to patch my shingles.

Ping ping.
Water drips in coffee cans.

Telephone rings.
Can't climb down
to answer now.

The machine tweaks
with messages.

O don't let tomorrow
be another day.

Pine Cones

With little pain you bear a daughter.
A golden child who loves you
as much as you love her.
She places her golden head in your lap.
She swings from the pine in a cut-out tire:
all of it meant to be.

Voices tell you the gods are jealous.
You ask, "Jealous of goodness?"
Once the doctor cut a half moon
in her eardrum.

Children arrive as pine cones.
You hold them on your lap, prickles or no.
The gods are fuming.

Your friends write her life
had meaning. Life was golden.
You see her descend the golden staircase.
The disease attacked her DNA.

People die in this plague,
flies in the eyes of African children.
In her wedding dress she lies
beneath a pine.

Marrakesh

Only their eyes showing,
camel drivers in blue turbans
have driven here with their carpets.
My guilt rides in on golden ponies,
gilds the minarets.
You asked me to make this journey
with you through the garden of Allah
open only on Fridays.
I chose to keep my prior appointment.
You kept your appointment.
Now I steal the memories
from the coins in the market,
from the eyes of the dead.

We would have hired the guide to shepherd us
through the market teeming
with mint, cilantro and roast chicken.

We would have found the herbalist
to cure you
and finally removed our veils
talking over our separation
which we both healed apart.
As it was, you rode the camel alone.
I kept the Christmas card.

Quick

Everyone else sees the dead.
Why not me?
Why can't you appear
as suicides do
to those they left abruptly?
Sit on the edge of my bed!

You keep beneath the surface,
in my lungs.
Sink or swim, I can't spit you out.

I've got you in the dead man's hold
but always underwater.
Come back just once.
Say, "This has to be quick."

Everyone else hears the dead.
Why don't I?
"Death knocks, but does not enter,"
my grandmother said
and even though she was deaf
(her hearing aid looked like a church)
she heard the knocking,
heard the procession of ancestors
file by her grandmother's coffin
in the front door, out the back.

That time you dialed
into my dream,
"I've got to take a trip
but the airport's closed."
I said, "I'll hang up now
to let someone else take care of you."
Was it then I let you go?

Everyone else touches the dead.
I wear the orchid you sent me.

When the postman rang
I wasn't home.
The orchid lay day after day in its box
until I claimed it.
Vampire, I lifted it out.

You completed your mission.
I don't need to be haunted.
We said goodbye.

Kernel

You hung in there,
kernel before the statue
of Bernardo O'Higgins.

You, out of ten thousand
bullmen rushed Europa.
You were mine.

You hung in there
with a hole in your heart.
That long bus trip,
Chile to Miami.

But every day your heart
bled
one or two drops.
I knew I would lose you
as later on I did.

You hung there
like a bat
until you were born.
I took your arms,
slid you to my groin while I
cut the cord.

Little by little
the vampire drew
out your blood
replaced it with bile.
Later on
I lost my child.

Missing You

David Oliveira

For Vichheka Thong and for the friends we miss together

David Oliveira

David Oliveira was born in Hanford and raised in Armona, towns about 35 miles south of Fresno in California's San Joaquin Valley. He currently lives in Santa Barbara.

His poems have appeared in numerous journals, including: *Americas Review, Art/Life, Café Solo, The Evergreen Chronicles, Poetry International* and *Verve*, and he is featured in the anthology *The Geography of Home* from Heyday Books.

He is the recipient of an Individual Artists award in poetry from the Santa Barbara Arts Fund, and his work has been nominated for a Puschcart Prize. He is the director of the Santa Barbara Poetry Series at the Contemporary Arts Forum. He is the publisher of Mille Grazie Press, which publishes a distinguished chapbook series featuring poets primarily from California's Central Coast, and *Poet Cards*, trading cards featuring poets instead of sports figures. He is also co-editor of *Solo*, a national journal of poetry.

It is not that I have lost more than anyone else, nor that my grief is deeper than others, nor that my losses have given me a special wisdom to impart, that has drawn me to write these poems. It seems to me that to display our grief publicly, to let the world see how sorry we are that our loved ones are gone, is a very important part of the human process of restoration and survival. That is why we ritualize funerals, hold memorial services out of the hearing of the praised. That is why I am inviting you now to witness my sadness for these dear loves.

— *David Oliveira*

Grief

For Chico Lusby

You will not believe me
when I tell you time will dry your tears—
that one day, not too many away from this one,
you will once more awaken to a morning full of plans—
that your body, which has lost its desire
for the flavor of melted cheese and toast,
will eat again, will discover
the new tastes of saffron and mangosteen—
that you will meet young women
whose quiet beauty will not remind you
of your sister's gentle face.
Already, you must suspect the way you feel now
is only the beginning of your sorrow.
Oh, you will walk on the beach again,
that much is certain, and you will rush home from work
excited to watch some team or other
get to their championship.
You will still find sunsets to admire,
and uncountable days will pass through you
which do not call out your sister's name.
But grief will surprise you,
even when you are no longer young,
stealing up from behind to touch your eyes
as you discover the familiar rhythms of her laugh
in the tap dance of the first drops
of the last spring rain against the windshield of your car.
No one else can know this sadness,
though in the world's slow unwrapping of days
such sadnesses walk with nearly everyone,
not every minute, to be sure,
but for enough minutes.

Portrait of a Late Summer Afternoon

Everyone in the picture is laughing,
looking away from the camera

as if delight is the nature
of human beings in each other's company

and what a person dropping by
at any odd hour, would discover,

coming to deliver a pizza
or borrow the afternoon paper

or join the teasing over September waistlines
and the unavoidable whim of lovers;

what would be happening
even if the photographer was not here

to save these friends exactly how
they ask to be remembered always.

Autumn

Because it is autumn,
I notice trees now, or rather,

I notice leaves—by their absence
and by the red and yellow stubbornness

which holds on to their limbs,
as though what a leaf is

disappears if they let go,
forgets in the slow descent,

the first warm breeze
that bent around the supple edges

before lifting their heart-shapes
to ride the air, like the birds,

until they believed the future was sky,
and there was nothing else to think.

Paso Robles, San Luis Obispo, San Luis Obispo

All our lives we've been told how things work.
Yet we persist in believing we barely age,
until some warm afternoon, we catch, by surprise,
a reflection in a store window,

hardly recognizing who we have become.
We take our turn at this, as if following
one another up a mountain without a clear trail,
our steps heavy from the need we carry

to be somewhere else,
some place we have never been,
and will not know when we arrive.
I think of a child's game played in the car

with my brothers and sisters as Dad drives
to the coast on Highway 41. Beverly
reads aloud a road sign, Paso Robles 45 miles,
and a hubcap falls off. At the next sign,

it's my turn. I say Paso Robles, then before
anything bad happens, Robert starts repeating
the line below, San Luis Obispo, San Luis Obispo,
and the hubcaps stay on. Never again

will any of us say Paso Robles without
adding two charms of San Luis Obispo;
towns we drive through on the way
to somewhere else, linked

in a small arsenal of protections
with Latin spells from mass.
We take it as our mission to say
the dangerous words at odd moments,

quickly adding the incantation that saves
someone from bad luck, a preemptive strike
to rid the world of another reason for sadness,
to let us be happy more often than we are.

The way a photograph of a picnic,
kept for years on the dresser, loses
subtle grays in the lawn, and the spread
of the blanket fades into dim folds

of someone's dress until only dark lines
marking the kindness of a smile, or
shadows proving the curve of an eye,
rise from yellowing distance into a face

beautiful beyond the burden of detail;
so small moments of glad luck
stand out in the picture I have become.
In the picture I dream of becoming,

on a beach, the smallest grain of sand visible
between my toes, watching the expanse of ocean
turn to the enormity of sky, there isn't
enough room for all the brown flights of sparrows

I want to remember. I want so much.
Desire hangs from my cheeks in the morning,
pulls with the weight of years; speaks my name
in the music of coffee, the traffic of work;

whispers at me in public places to let my eyes
call to passing faces which don't stop.
Today want follows me as I'm driving
along those same highways of childhood.

Each road sign now points to a place
where I'm missing a friend; and
I want to be like these hills, which are just hills,
skins of straw blades mining August light

for their splendor—no thoughts of travelers
or the roads where every turn is a sadness for someone.
I say I want to go first, but in truth,
I don't want any of us to go at all.

Foolish wants of a person no smarter than myself.
Like magic words, the few tricks I've learned
that charm the universe to my side
to keep pain at bay, only work when they work,

and there remain unavoidable moments
in the elegance of days passing between
light and dark, when hurt is all I can do.

Mary's Name

You study his face for something familiar,
one distinctive feature that names
the man I've brought to your door.
It's all right this time.
He's my friend, someone you've never met.

Mornings are easy.
Coffee is hot water and Hills Brothers.
Laundry is Tide and once-worn clothes.
The rest of the day moves among
the faces of people you know and places
where you've put things for keeping;
names meandering over the same roads
you've taken to old age, so scattered
you'll have to learn them again.

The doctor calls it anomia, the way
the attributes of things are stored
by the brain apart from their names;
the place that keeps Mary separate
from the place which holds the exact brown
of her iris, separate from where
a reason explains the small sadness
in the music of her laugh.

I suppose there is a time when
nothing has a name,
the stars simply lights in our eyes.

Are there many stars out tonight?

Why David, darling,
all the stars are out tonight.

The Fairness of Life

For Ron Teschner

When I am with you it is I who am dying.
It is my breath choking in the goodness
of air through plastic tubes.
It is my arms too weak to help me sit up,
my head, swimming in morphine,
unable to resolve
the actuarial math of life:
father dead at 67, grandmother at 56,
and me, as close to my number as you to yours,
lots of good parts still working.
We never talk about pain,
you with too much
and I with none that matters.
I'm caught in your hurry to
get on with it, like the child
afraid of being sent to bed before
getting the dessert he was promised.
We get what we get—a body
to collect the single days we are given
or minutes, when a day is too much,
a body which grows plain and unnoticed
or beautiful and pursued,
or grows old and unfamiliar to the hands
washing its loose cover of skin,
or doesn't grow at all.
And we get this moment, of course,
all of this moment.

Potluck at Katherine Hepburn's

For Clifford Olson

It isn't really
to Katherine Hepburn's
we are going, though
you insist
I cook my best dish
as if it was.
There will be plenty of time
to be ordinary,
you tell me,
after the worms take
the last worry
from our faces.

In this world
there are many parties,
most of which
we are not invited to.
Ordinary persons go
to ordinary parties,
sit outside
the conversation
close to the wine and chips,
have someone else's
way with words
until it's time to go.

You never go
to an ordinary party,
usually arriving ahead of
President Carter, in time
to introduce
Aretha to Mother Teresa;
and when the Dalai Lama
forgets the punch line to
the joke he's telling Liz Taylor,
it's you, there, in the middle,
whose every gesture is followed
to the end of the story.

The art of entertaining,
you often say, is to be the host
at other people's parties,
a guest at your own.
As a good host
would always suggest a dish
to bring to the potluck,
so a good guest
would be remiss
in not bringing a dish
befitting the host
who has such famous friends.

How You Talk

For Dave Williams

You don't always talk of wind or rain
or flowers blooming against desert odds
or how pine trees determine the mountain
or Earth's vanity on summer beaches.
Sometimes you talk about me—finding
enough in my life like your life
to feel safe with ordinary expressions of affection,
finding enough difference to keep
our conversations a whisper, until
the shyness moves from our more familiar natures,
finding uncommon words to tell our common stories,
brief elegant narratives to explain
the reach of our hands from childhood until now.
But your most eloquent words are silent,
saved to talk about yourself,
said in the firm hold of your embrace,
or when you close your eyes to face the pain
coming too often to mention each time,
or in the uneven turn of your smile,
that always says goodbye,
like good friends do,
as though we should see each other again.

Someone Else

For Allen Schindler, Matthew Shepard, in memoriam

Who doesn't look into a mirror
hoping to find someone else,
and all of us, more or less, the same—
so much water and fat,
so many proteins and minerals.
Yet it's our differences which
stare back from the family portrait.
Even the child knows what
will be disappointing in the adult.
It isn't until we are dead
that we finally look alike.
Fingers which once pointed in derision
rest as aimlessly as fingers
that once arranged roses. Mouths that
spat on the waking hours of those
from whom they'd stolen sleep,
lie as quietly as the mouths which
kissed away the children's
fear of thunder. Hands that tore
the living heart from those
who only had a breath
between themselves and nothing,
hold as much as hands that reached out
to comfort the crying around them.
Feet which kicked every bone
of a head until the face shattered
beyond recognition, share the same
slumber as feet which carried
life to love and wonder.
It's all here, all we start with,
all we come to, all laid out
in a common meal for
the undiscriminating appetites
swarming to the table
without manners, without waste.

Bruised Boxes

We do it so often it seems routine—
collecting pieces of friends lives into
plastic garbage bags and cardboard boxes,
involving ourselves in the hard work of
finally getting their lives together.
We study each object as carefully
as dispassionate critics assigning
lasting values to eclectic good taste.
Here, an old photo kept casually
in a shoe box with a few pennies and
last year's canceled checks—just forgotten trash
to be tossed with empty cans and rotting
fruit, or a treasured memento of a
dear lover remembered beyond the brief
affair, or a priceless artifact of
our time, saved to unlock the mysteries
of modern civilization to an
unsuspecting future generation.
Stacking the decisions in our favor,
we carefully disperse the goods among
family, friends, and usual strangers
spending weekend mornings paying respects
to the precious bargains of a lifetime.
We hold up a bruised box, shaking loose some
last grey speck, watching it fall silently
into the mix of blood, dirt, dust and sweat,
making the primordial mud on which
we have taken such a civilized stand.
Finding new ash indistinguishable
from battered old ground, we lose you again,
losing ourselves in tight emotions and
diminishing memories struggling
to keep track of all the scattered pieces.
It will have to be someone else to put
you back together now—someone brighter
who can keep all the details straight without
getting confused by your frivolous charm,

someone with a new archaeology
that can reconstruct personalities
by tracing the scent of their passion through
the weary work they leave behind—someone
with stamina to search from door to door,
buying back your things sold without thinking—
someone with patience to keep sitting, like
the old god of our fathers on the day
of judgment, sifting through piles of dirt
for the last particle of human dust.

Missing You

For Rathana Touch

The world ends one person at a time.

You are dead.
Today this wants to be the most important thing
that ever happened between us.

Strange to feel surprise
        when we both knew it would come to this,

me standing over dead you...

each immaculately groomed strand of hair...dead,
    the Chinese opera in your mouth...dead,
        your sinuous waltzing strut...dead,
            both flirting eyelashes...dead,
                hands empty of rice...dead,
                    stubborn brow...dead,
                        Adam's apple...dead,
                            fingerprints...dead,
                                belly button...dead,
            elbows, shins, earlobes, nipples, asshole,
                dead, dead, dead, dead, dead,

...or you standing over dead me.

Though you are dead,
                    let me tell you anyway,
this is not the most important thing between us.
This silence doesn't have the scope
of the fight we had over that something
                                you never explained to me,
some insensitive thing I did, or didn't do.
Sentenced to a year of civility.

Nor are you more quiet at this moment
than when sneaking into the kitchen at night.
You never stopped eating.
Even now, I don't understand how you were thin.

You are dead,
and this morning we all beat you to the food,
all the old friends gathered here
to tell how you are missed,

one of us the unlucky one who lives long enough
to miss everybody.

The Business of Canaries

For Jerry White

I

Once miners followed
canaries into
their work, commanding
sweeps of song into
the breaking darkness.
Setting the cages
against the rock, they
listened beyond their
natural love or
inclination for
avian music,
beyond the luring
melodies calling
out to memories
of the sun outside,
beyond their innate
dislike for the taste
of dust in their mouths.
Their listening tuned
in to the silence.
Their attention fixed
to the still spaces,
anticipating
each next note that would
allow them again
a safe turn to a
miner's dark business.
And the business of
canaries? To sing
their sweet tunes until
the poison gases
attack their short breath,
and a bird's own high
metabolism
turns against its best
interest to choke

the song back into
its bewildered throat—
alarming miners
with the news that no
sacrifice can be
considered too small.

II

Gently, I touch my
friend, putting my hands
on the curve of his
shoulder, my fingers
moving back and forth
across the expanse
of that tender skin,
searching for just one
path around the pain.
"Tell me where it hurts,"
I say, knowing all
the time exactly
where. It hurts on the
beach when the setting
sun turns on city
lights, capturing the
first breath of twilight
for old lovers who
hold each other's hand
without first thinking
about city or light
or moments moving
from their reach. It hurts
at the movies when
we can't find our queer
lives on the screen,
as if faggots have no
sorrow deep enough,
nor love rich enough,
to be worth talking
about in the light.
It hurts at home as
we pace carefully

around the limits
of our living room
anxious to be out,
confident we won't
get lost in the crowd,
where there are always
plenty of people
who will help us find
our place. And it hurts,
my friend, here, where you're
sitting, cold and wet,
in your own shit, not
yet ready to scream
the indignation
that your body is
on its own, leaving
home without you, and
leaving you without
losing even one
recognizable
measure of manhood.

III

The day never seems
to turn on good news
anymore. This day
has brought another
precious name which I
must dutifully
record into the
halting memory
that has become a
living chronicle
of my good people.
This is my business—
remembering friends
whose dear lives were a
brief risk for beauty.
It is my business
to ask you to break
through the noise and shit

of generations
until it's your voice
choking on the songs
of a lifetime—your
lungs scratching for sweet
breath in the poisoned
sky of history—
until, suddenly
alarmed, you stop
working and remember
my good people too.

Reporter (from Storytelling)

For Morris Kight

It is morning, again,
only yourself in the yard,
serving a breakfast
of water to the garden—
each tree and bush,
the namesake of someone
loved and gone, touching you
in their shade, caressing
the solitude until you're resting,
hardly alone, among friends.
The silver eucalyptus
is for Steve, dying when
his heart became too tired
to run after another step.
How long since we stopped
expecting someone might
die simply because the body
finished everything it could,
some part wearing out,
in this time when no one
simply dies anymore?
More certain was a ficus
you planted for Sheldon,
and another for Ken,
after months watching
their bodies slowly melt
to the bone—the universe,
itself, shrinking around them,
becoming so small,
all that was left could be seen
from their beds. For David you
placed an Arizona cypress
beside the magnolia
he helped plant for someone else,
learning from him how to be
the expert botanist
who discerns Southern

California seasons
from subtle changes
of color and mood
in your plants—memorizing
their classification
in the soft cadence of Latin.
Pneumocystis carinii.
Mycobacterium avium.
Kaposi's sarcoma.
Esophageal candidiasis.
Cytomegalovirus.
Tonight, your sleep will
bring you back to the garden,
to dig, like a mole,
in the dark, pushing
dirt away with your hands
from holes coaxed out
of earth's living skin.
You plant a pine this time,
something tall and slender
as the friend it recalls.
I follow you
with buckets of blood
to wet the thirsty roots.
We work toward morning,
running out of ground
before running out of trees,
running out of sleep before
determining what is the dream
and what is the world.
At sunrise, we stand in a forest
listening to the trees
tell us their names.

How Good Fortune Surprises Us

Jackson Wheeler

For Ruth, Maxine, Marianne, Polly, Dave, Dan, Pat and Doug

Jackson Wheeler

Jackson Wheeler was born and raised in Andrews, North Carolina in Southern Appalachia. He attended the University of North Carolina at Chapel Hill, and attended graduate school in California.

His work has appeared in many journals and magazines. He is the author of one book of poetry, *Swimming Past Iceland* (Mille Grazie Press) and is co-editor of the distinguished journal of poetry, *Solo*. Since 1990, he has directed the Arcade Poetry Series, a monthly reading series featuring the best poets of Southern California. He is also the founder and co-director of the Ventura Poetry Festival.

He is currently a health and wellness manager for the Tri-Counties Regional Center, serving individuals with mental retardation, autism, cerebral palsy and epilepsy.

Most of these poems were written in response to one loss or another, primarily my brother Joseph's death from complications of AIDS. As such, they are purely articulations of individual grief which acknowledge the bonds linking all humanity to the emotions of loss, that *near country*.

—*Jackson Wheeler*

El Dia de los Muertos

If the dead know anything at all
that we do not...

it is a long forgetting.

And if by custom
they gather on the turn
of the year, at the edge of life,

who notices their silent waving,
all their gestures of Hello

and Goodbye?

How Good Fortune Surprises Us

I was hauling freight
out of the Carolinas
up to the Cumberland Plateau
when, in Tennessee, I saw
from the freeway, at 2 am
a house ablaze.

Water from the firehoses arced
into luminescent rainbows.

The only sound, the dull roar of my truck
passing. I found myself strangely happy.
It was misfortune on that cold night
falling on someone's house,
but not mine
not mine.

Florence, Oregon, 1978

For Belle & John

Air fragrant with wood smoke,
killdeer hugging the shore,
somewhere in the sad confusion of driftwood
a radio plays Copeland.

Aunt Belle is up ahead, walking.
She told me that the family has misremembered
the important dates of the oxen trek
across Tatham Gap in the Great Smokies.
"It was later, about five years later."

I have thought about this business of "later."
She is the last of my father's family
to have memories, and she doesn't remember.

Ah, God, I brought his ghost this far,
to this shore of dark pine, and now
I let it go, a fist-sized grief, mute, for
I have forgotten the sound of his voice.

I turn into the wind because
there is nothing more I can say or do.

"Go home, Daddy. It's late now."

At Fifty

How did I come here;
awash in a sea of prescriptions,
on first name basis with all
the hospital orderlies from here
to there, and back again?

There is a photograph somewhere
of a younger woman, me at a sadder
time, full of anger and suicide,
standing in a garden in Santa Barbara
long since bulldozed into memory.

It is a metaphor I cling to,
the bulldozer, like Noah's flood
the Second Coming
the Titanic going down filled
with the idle rich.

There is something decisive about
a bulldozer. I could see Eve rearranging
the garden, clearing a space for a tract
house with a pool. What good is a tree
of knowledge when you need a roof over your head?

Did Jesus use a bulldozer to dig up Lazarus
sweeping in from the edge of town with tears
in his eyes? There are days I feel resurrected,
bulldozed awake, to the beep, beep
of the IV drip, back for another metaphor.

For Carol at the End of Summer

Carol Chandlee 7/21/38 - 8/17/97

I

I've been thinking about you all day.
El Niño has brought a hint of rain,
clouds piling up all afternoon. Here
on the edge of the continent the Pacific
is four shades of blue! Brown Pelicans
dive and swoop, dive and swoop
busy as tailors stitching sky to sea,
making a hem of the horizon.

II

Cat owners become accustomed
to the strangled cry of fledglings
or whisp of lizard dropped
at their feet, gifts of devotion.
It's enough to make us wonder
how we thought it possible to get
through life without being startled by love.

III

Carol, thinking of you gone
here at the end of summer
is more than my heart can bear,
so for this moment let me imagine
you with your beloved Marianne
some place exotic, the South Island of New Zealand,
near Dunedin, on the fairway of a perfect course,
in bright sun. A snapshot postcard.

Wish you were here.

For Glenn

I
The last time we talked, you stood
among the lavenders and sages
at the local nursery, extolling
the fine points of gardening
in a desert; an appreciation
for the exotic colors drought tolerant
plants can produce.
You were taking Chinese herbs, bitter melon,
felt good you said, though tired most days,
saving your energy for the important things:
your garden, painting, dinner with family.
We watched a couple walk by with something
large and extravagant, needing a Mono Lake's
worth of water to survive. "Well," you said,
"it is beautiful, if impractical." And isn't
the love between two men a struggle, like
finding a plant worth all the water to make it bloom.

II
When I walk into the gallery
among the landscapes of your last year,
Topa Topa, South Mountain, Wheeler Canyon,
I find myself in clear October light
waiting for you to step into the room.

III
You were a seismograph, measuring
the slippages and jolts of our reaction
to your illness.

Glenn, your death diminishes us; all these deaths
diminish us, carrying off the witnesses
to our ineptitude, till no one is left to remember
how we were afraid, failed our obligation to heal
while watching so many die. In time, if no one remembers
what we have done or were unable to do, it will be a mercy.

Directions in Decatur

From Third Avenue, to East Lake Boulevard,
to Ponce de Leon, to Peachtree Street,
to Linden Avenue. This is the way
to the hospital. We would know it
in our sleep.

It is the map of our present life.
To make you well, I would walk
this route over broken glass,
each footprint, incarnadine, a STOP
sign.

Sweeney's Encampment

(historical marker, McClendon Ave, Atlanta, GA)

It is the one historical marker
on McClendon Ave I did not read
regarding the Civil War, or if I did,
I forgot.

It is on the edge of a park in the neighborhood
known as Lake Claire, near Little Five Points,
on the way to downtown, on the way to where
you worked.

I think Sweeney was part of Sherman's Army;
forgive me if I've gotten it wrong,
but what was left of your life
filled every moment
of mine.

The drive through Lake Claire was a shortcut
you showed me. If I knew then what I know now
I would have taken the longest way around,
stopped at every marker of great or
little significance.

I would have insisted we both get out of the car,
fingered the raised letters on each bronze marker
read the inscriptions out loud—consigned it all to memory—
the historical fact, you, me, and the failing light of
late September.

At the Emory Eye Clinic

In the lobby, plush with gray and purple chairs
we sit among old people,
children with one eye bandaged
and the young men with AIDS,
blind or nearly so with CMV.

Your implant has worked well—a beacon of sorts
for the stunned and immobilized. Ironic, you
see well, although your damaged brain is already
leaking away all the words you have for the world.
In the elevator you asked me where we were.

Across from us, two young men drawn and wasted.
One reaches with spectral hand and brushes the hair
back from his companion's face, not once but two
or three times as if to say, "Look honey, we're in this
together, I'm here."

Instinctively, I take your hand.

Joseph at Huntington Gardens

It is near winter in Decatur,
if you were well I would
take you to San Marino, the lush
enclave near Pasadena, escort you
through the Huntington Gardens
up to the Tea House and the raked
gravel of the Zen Garden, where we
would contemplate: the mysteries of three maples,
rocks which are both mountain and island,
the perfection of bonsai.

Tell me, is it true that death
distills this world into one place
that is everywhere and here in the same breath?
I want to believe, Joseph, when I look at the red-orange
Moon Bridge, its reflection in the water completing
the perfect O of eternity, that you and I are seeing
it with the same eyes, that I feel your breath
hear your excited whisper, "Look, look!"

How Fever Transforms Us

It was the last night of your life.
You had abandoned language.
Your body was full of fever:

like a night in August,
like a bonfire, consuming
the very air in the room of your unmaking.
In your presence, in the absence of air,
what do I breathe brother,
other than silence?
What do I breathe?

The Office of Love

Keeping you dry has become
the work of Sisyphus.
I change you five times a night, sometimes more.

Unable to speak about how your body has engaged
itself in a great civil war, you are the face of resignation.
Your eyes and hands joined the rebellion

last week, surrendering all hope.
I talk you through everything:
"I'm going to change you now."

"Here, let me cover you up."
"This will only take a minute."
Some nights I tell you over and over that I love you

believing that hearing is the last of the senses to go, thinking
you might die at any moment, wanting you to leave
knowing at least that much.

Swimming Past Iceland

For Joseph Wheeler

I have been told that people
with pneumonia drown. So I
imagine him swimming away.

I buy freesias for his room,
bring a perfect nest
blown from the olive tree.
Does it belong to a shrike or phoebe?

My brother does not answer.
He is swimming, they tell me,
somewhere near the horizon,
nearly out of sight.

I spend the afternoon
cooking lentils, baking bread.
Perhaps he will swim back
for dinner, wet and hungry.

I smooth his sheets, read,
imagine him out in the dark.
I am afraid to wade after him.
Is he cold, I wonder.

I put my ear to his lips.
Breath rasps in time with his strokes.
As a child, he threatened
to swim to England.

In last night's fevered dream
he cleared the coast of Labrador,
Greenland by dawn. He awakes smiling.
"Ice," he says.

I put ice to his lips.
He is hot and cold
like Iceland in the children's
book about volcanoes.

He paces himself.
Almost there.
"Home," he says
off the coast of Iceland.

He is exhausted.
Even in my dream,
waist deep
in the icy cold,

he has made Iceland.
Passed it.
Too exhausted for England.
Too tired to return.

He is drowning out there, spent swimmer,
off some distant coast
after all the stragglers
and generations caught sleeping

in hospitals
next to the bed
of someone with pneumonia
drowning, dying, dreaming.

Someone who swims from
one fevered place to another,
but never home.